Green MEDICINE

JOURNAL BOOK

LORI HARRINGTON

WestBow Press books may be ordered through booksellers or by contacting:

WestBow Press
A Division of Thomas Nelson & Zondervan
1663 Liberty Drive
Bloomington, IN 47403
www.westbowpress.com
844-714-3454

ISBN: 978-1-6642-9110-2 (sc)
ISBN: 978-1-6642-9111-9 (e)

Print information available on the last page.

WestBow Press rev. date: 03/02/2023

WESTBOW
PRESS®
A DIVISION OF THOMAS NELSON
& ZONDERVAN

PREFACE

I write this on what has been now marked as a very special day for me. I was baptized this day—October 23, 2022—at ChangePoint Church in Anchorage, Alaska. I was saved at the young age of five. I don't remember the exact date, but I know it was a Sunday and I was sitting in the second pew with my family. After listening to the pastor's sermon, as I had numerous times before, I remember being very moved and wanting to have Jesus in my heart. I started to cry a little. My mother noticed and asked if I wanted to be saved. I nodded and said, "Yes." We walked hand in hand to a side room to the right of the choir stage. There, we got down on our knees and she walked me through saying the sinner's prayer. This memory is as clear as if I were there right now.

I am not a perfect person. There has definitely been unforeseen complications in becoming who I am today. I have made some terrible mistakes. I have made some very bad choices. I have done and said a few things I not only regret, but wish with my whole heart that I could undo if I could. Not to make excuses for myself or anyone, but I would venture to say that most people would say the same things about themselves. I don't go to church and study God's word because I am a perfect person who is better than anyone else; it's because I'm not. Ruth Bell Graham had written on her gravestone "End of Construction. Thank you for your patience." Likewise, I think of myself as a long work in progress. To me, a lot of it has been unplanned. For God, I am sure not all I have experienced is what He wanted for me. I took side trips along this journey when I should have stuck to the route I was shown to travel. However, I am sure, despite choices I made on my own because of what I thought was best for me at the time, God has been using everything in my life for His good. I know He will continue to work with me the remainder of the way.

I was always encouraged to be baptized when I was a child but not pushed to do so. It isn't a requirement of being saved. The emphasis on its importance seemed to fall to the wayside with the disruptions in my home life. However, in the months leading up to my decision to be baptized as an adult, the topic kept coming up in various things I read and things I listened to. I could hear God speaking to me quietly that this needed to be done. We are commanded to do so and it symbolizes a change inside.

The process for baptism at my church is to take a short class a few weeks before to understand what baptism is. You learn about why you should be baptized and what to expect the day of the event. You select your service, answer some questions on a form, and provide a faith statement. I selected my husband to read my faith statement and one of the church elders did the honors of the baptism. The day of, I became quite nervous, and the vanity of a middle-aged woman kicked in as I sat waiting for my turn to stand before the congregation. When my name was called, all that faded away. All I could hear was my husband reading my words and the pastor saying I was baptized in the name of the Father, the Son, and the Holy Spirit. I am left with a feeling of pure joy in my heart. I know this comes from obeying God. If you have not been baptized, I hope you consider doing so soon. Study, think, then obey.

On a cloudless, blue-sky, cold fall day, my *Green Medicine* came in the form of complete obedience to God by being immersed in His love.

This is my faith statement, read on the day of my baptism.

> I was 5 years old when Pastor Olsen's sermon at Calvary Baptist Church in Chillicothe, Illinois, reached my young heart. On my knees with my mother, I prayed the sinner's prayer and accepted Jesus as my Savior. At times, I struggled and questioned my faith, but now at 56, I know without doubt that God loves me, and His Son died for my sin. I am grateful for parents who grounded me at a young age in God's Word.

> God, it's been a long time coming, but I'm here to share with everyone in my baptism that I follow Jesus.

INTRODUCTION

A majority of the years I had with my father, there was a common thread running through our conversations that God gave us the world of nature to soothe our souls and ground us in knowing He is all around us in His creation. All our rivers of communication flowed back to what my father dubbed as "God's *Green Medicine*."

Our parents are just as human and flawed as we, ourselves, are. They love us, raise us, care for us, lift us up with things they say and do, and send us sideways off the rails for the same reasons. Hurtful things said and done can linger a lifetime. I just can't hang on to any anger. I have found life more rewarding and productive by letting go of any resentment. I know both my parents loved me and did the best they could, just like I am doing in my own life. Everything that has happened in my life has led me to where I am now, and I think that's a good place to be.

My dad was not a perfect man. We had our differences at times. We had wonderful times together as well and I loved him dearly. I choose to go with all the good memories, as there were so many. He was an inspiration to me. He taught me to have a foundation in Christ and how to learn more about God through His creation. I am very thankful and blessed for this.

> Because what may be known of God is manifest in them for God has known it to them. For since the creation of the world His invisible attributes are clearly seen, being understood by the things that are made, even His eternal power and Godhead, so that they are without excuse.
> —Romans 1: 19–20 (NKJV)

HOW TO USE THIS JOURNAL

This guided journal is a companion to the *Green Medicine* book, giving you the opportunity to put pen to paper on your own thoughts and experiences of God's creation. It would, of course, be best to read the corresponding entry in the *Green Medicine* book. This will help get your mind in gear for thinking about similar situations in your own life and motivate you with additional inspiring pictures and verses.

Each numbered entry in this journal follows the correlating subject matter of the entry in the *Green Medicine* book. As you follow along in this companion book, think of your own comparable life events and write about them as you meditate on God's word. Let each one move you to journal your own thoughts and experiences. Allow yourself to get closer to Him.

There is no deadline or requirement to finish this in any particular timeframe. There's no regime in which you spend your time reading or journaling either. It can be on a high cliff after a strenuous hike, a break on a beach while kayaking, or on your couch, curled up with a cup of tea on a rainy day. The main goal is to reflect on God's word as you soak up the *Green Medicine* in the beauty of His creation that surrounds you.

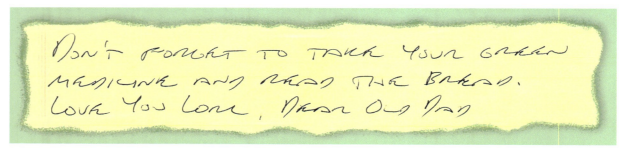

Don't forget to take your green medicine and read the Bible. Love you Lots, Dear Old Dad

TIGER LILY FESTIVAL
Trusting God Will Take Care of You

Consider the lilies of the field, how they grow; they toil not.
—Matthew 6:28 (ASV)

My father created the Tiger Lily Festival for me and my brother because he loved the orange flowers that grew wild in the countryside ditches of Illinois. Yes, it was for fun as well as an excuse to get ice cream treats to celebrate. However, it was founded in the Bible where God says he will take care of us just as he does the flowers (Matthew 6:28 ASV). It is easy to be caught up in the turmoil and concerns of the day. It's not wrong to plan and prepare, but the flowers of the world are a reminder God will take care of you.

Dogwood blossom, Gatlinburg, Tennessee

Are not two sparrows sold for a penny? Yet not one of them will fall to the ground outside your Father's care. And even the very hairs of your head are all numbered. So don't be afraid; you are worth more than many sparrows.
—Matthew 10:29–31 (NIV)

_____

_____

_____

_____

Great are the works of the Lord; they are pondered by all who delight in them. Glorious and majestic are his deeds, and his righteousness endures forever. He has caused his wonders to be remembered; the Lord is gracious and compassionate.
—Psalm 111:2–4 (NIV)

3

FRIENDLY CONNECTIONS
Making the Connection to God with the Nature around You

🍃🍃🍃

By the word of the Lord, the heavens were made. And all the host of them by the breath of His mouth. He gathers the waters of the sea together as a heap; He lays up the deep in storehouses. Let all the earth fear the Lord; Let all the inhabitants of the world stand in awe of Him.
—Psalm 33:6–8 (NKJV)

A close friend brought Romans 1:19–20 (NKJV) to my attention, pointing out how God makes himself known to all through creation. Our days can be hectic and full of the routines of life. Do you stop to see the natural beauty around you? Are you taking time to see God's *Green Medicine* each day?

Clouds rolling over mountains at sunset, Clingman's Dome Road, Great Smoky Mountains National Park, Tennessee

_____

_____

_____

_____

_____

_____

_____

🍃🍃🍃

Lift up your eyes on high, And see who has created these things, Who brings out their host by number; He calls them all by name, By the greatness of His might and the strength of His power; not one is missing.
—Isaiah 40:26 (NKJV)

IN THE BEGINNING
You Are Valuable and a Part of God's Creation

In the beginning God created the heavens and the earth.
—Genesis 1:1 (NKJV)

One can feel small in the grand scheme of things when looking at the night sky or standing before a huge mountain range or looking at the ocean. I find myself awestruck that God created all He has. He is in control of the smallest of details. Sometimes, looking at the bigger picture of what is going on in the world can evoke the same feeling. It's easy to feel insignificant. You are not. Let yourself be filled with that wonder while taking comfort in the fact that you are one of the important details in the world God created.

Haines Highway at Dezadeash Lake, the Yukon Territory, Canada

----

For thus says the Lord, Who created the heavens, Who is God, Who formed the earth and made it, Who has established it, Who did not create it in vain, Who formed it to be inhabited; "I am the Lord, and there is no other."
—Isaiah 45:18 (NKJV)

DRIVING TO ALASKA
The Events That Have Inspired You for Great Journeys into the Depths of God's Creation

A man's heart plans his way, but the Lord directs his steps.
—Proverbs 16:9 (NKJV)

One of the biggest, most unique experiences of my life was driving the Alcan (Alaska-Canadian) Highway when I first moved to Alaska. Most people have some notable adventure that accentuates an experience in nature. It doesn't have to be a 5,000-mile drive across two countries. For some, a family camping trip or special vacation is an exceptional memory. What are yours? Remember them here, or write about where you are right now.

Alaska Highway heading east out of Whitehorse, Yukon, at Takhini-Burn Rest Area, Canada

_____
_____
_____
_____
_____
_____
_____
_____
_____

Lead me in Your truth and teach me, For You are the God of my salvation. On you I wait all the day.
—Psalm 25:5 (NKJV)

SALT OF THE EARTH
Be the Salt of the Earth to Bring Good Flavor to the Lives of Others

❧ ❧ ❧

You are the salt of the earth; but if the salt loses its flavor, how shall it be seasoned? It is then
good for nothing but to be thrown out and trampled underfoot by men.
—Matthew 5:13 (NKJV)

God says we are to be the salt of the Earth that brings out the flavor of God in all things so all can taste a well-
seasoned life. Bringing the right balance of flavor to those you cross paths with can be challenging. I know
I am a work in progress, but I try diligently to bring the positive and good taste of God to others.

Fishing boat heading out of boat harbor in Kachemak Bay, Homer, Alaska

_____

_____

_____

_____

_____

_____

_____

_____

_____

❧ ❧ ❧

Salt is good, but if the salt loses its flavor, how will you season it? Have salt in yourselves, and have peace with one another.
—Mark 9:50 (NKJV)

STILL WATERS
Have You Found the Still Waters God Provides to Bring Calm to Your Life No Matter What You Are Going Through?

He leadeth me beside still waters, he restoreth my soul. He leadeth me in the paths of righteousness for His name's sake..
—Psalm 23:2–3 (KJV)

One of the favorite trails I hiked in the Great Smoky Mountains National Park was in an area called Greenbrier. The unmarked trail was dubbed the Rhododendron Trail by locals, but it was known more for its numerous, small, scenic waterfalls in the stream the trail paralleled. It was a route of tranquility for me and still reminds me of Psalm 23 (NKJV). Write about your "still water" places that bring you peace of mind.

Mountain stream along Roaring Fork Motor Nature Trail, Great Smoky Mountains National Park, Tennessee

_____

_____

_____

_____

_____

_____

_____

_____

_____

_____

Boat returning to boat harbor in Portage Cove, Haines, Alaska

When you pass through the waters, I will be with you; and when you pass through the rivers, they will not sweep over you. When you walk through the fire, you will not be burned; the flames will not set you ablaze.
—Isaiah 43:2 (NIV)

QUIET CONFIDENCE
Peace That Only God Can Bring to Your Life

God is our refuge and strength, a very present help in trouble. Therefore, we will not fear, even
though the earth be removed and though the mountains be carried into the midst of the sea:
though its waters roar and be troubled, though the mountains shake with its swelling.
—Psalm 46:1–3 (NKJV)

I enjoy people watching. The Vietnam Veterans Memorial Wall, better known as just "The Wall," is quite the
place to engage in this activity. The reactions of those visiting the area can be very emotional. I've been there
twice, and on one occasion, I observed a young man's grief as he found the name of a friend he apparently
had lost in the war. Many people carry deep heartache with them. I have some of my own. But we all can
be confident that God embraces us and provides the strength to carry us through painful loss.

Rainbow over Chilkoot Inlet, Haines, Alaska

_____

_____

_____

_____

_____

No, in all these things we are more than conquerors through him who loved us. For I am convinced that neither death
nor life, neither angels nor demons, neither the present nor the future, nor any powers, neither height nor depth, nor
anything else in all creation, will be able to separate us from the love of God that is in Christ Jesus our Lord.
—Romans 8:37–39 (NIV)

EXPERIENCE OF LIGHT
Touching the Lives of Others by Letting Them See the Light of God Shining through You

You are the light of the world. A town built on a hill cannot be hidden. Neither do people light a lamp and put it under a bowl. Instead they put it on its stand, and it gives light to everyone in the house. In the same way, let your light shine before others, that they may see your good deeds and glorify your Father in heaven.
—Matthew 5:14–16 (NIV)

The aurora borealis, or northern lights, can be seen in the dark skies of Alaska and other locations in the Northern Hemisphere from early fall to early spring. The intensity and color can vary, but they are always a showstopper for anyone witnessing them. We are to be like the aurora for God in the lives of others. Your level of intensity may vary from giving a mere smile to a passerby to stepping up to help someone in need at a difficult time. What ways are you letting God shine through you?

Northern lights over mountains, Haines, Alaska

Sunset view from Clingman's Dome, Great Smoky Mountains National Park, Tennessee

Indeed My hand has laid the foundation of the earth, And My right hand has stretched
out the heavens; When I call to them, they stand up together.
— Isaiah 48:13 (NKJV)

DO NOT WORRY
You Matter To God. Let Go of Worry and Trust Him.

✿✿✿

Look at the birds of the air; they do not sow or reap or store away in barns, and yet your heavenly Father feeds them.
Are you not much more valuable than they? Can any one of you by worrying add a single hour to your life? …
But seek first His kingdom and His righteousness, and all these things will be given to you as well. Therefore do
not worry about tomorrow, for tomorrow will worry about itself. Each day has enough trouble of its own.
— Matthew 6:26–27 and 33–34 (NIV)

We have a couple of bird feeders at our home. We love watching the various type of birds flutter around, taking their
turns to peck away at the food source we provide. Although they are capable of foraging on their own, they seem to
know we will set out more for them when the supply is getting low. It's a sin to worry because you are not trusting
God to provide what you need. Worry is immobilizing; concern moves you into action. As you work through your
day and trying times, be assured God knows your needs and will be your steady calm for what you require in life.

Raven along Chilkat River, Haines, Alaska

_____

_____

_____

_____

_____

_____

✿✿✿

Casting all your care upon Him, for He cares for you.
—1 Peter 5:7 (NKJV)

GREATER FROM SORROW

Be Grounded in God and Take Comfort Knowing He Will Use All Circumstances for His Greater Purpose

Now may the God of hope fill you with all joy and peace in believing, that
you may abound in hope by the power of the Holy Spirit.
— Romans 15:13 (NKIV)

At some point, everyone questions why bad things happen to good people. I think everyone knows of those so undeserving of what happens to them. It can be hard to understand. But as Romans 8:28 says, "God causes all things to work together for good to those who are called according to *His* purpose" (NASB). When your heart is broken, you can submerge yourself in the *Green Medicine* God provides in His creation to comfort you. This life is not where it ends if you are a Christian, but God will hold you up here on earth.

Blue Spider Wort blossom, Greenbrier area of the Great Smoky Mountains National Park, Tennessee

_____
_____
_____
_____
_____
_____
_____
_____
_____
_____

Denali and the Alaska Range in Fall, Denali National Park, Alaska

You shall increase my greatness and comfort me on every side.
— Psalm 71:21 (NKJV)

GOD'S POCKET
You Are Always Wrapped up in God's Love and Strength—Where Do You Find God's Pocket?

Shout for Joy, you heavens; rejoice, you earth; burst into song, you mountains! For the
Lord comforts his people and will have compassion on his afflicted ones.
— Isaiah 49:13 (NIV)

The sudden loss of a friend and colleague years ago made me realize how precious life is. Making the most
of your time and not taking life for granted should be an undertone to each day. You only get one life to
live, so don't waste opportunities. My friend's final resting place was in an ocean cove called God's Pocket,
where she and her husband frequently kayaked. I think there are God pockets tucked away in nature all
over this world to give us rest we need as we journey through our life on earth. Where are yours?

Humpback whales near Resurrection Bay, Seward, Alaska

Starfish on shores of Fox Island, Resurrection Bay, Seward, Alaska

I will both lie down in peace, and sleep; For You alone, O Lord, make me dwell in safety.
— Psalm 4:8 (NKJV)

FOCUSED FOR THE JOURNEY
Keep Your Focus on God As You Travel Through Life

In the Morning, Lord, you hear my voice; in the morning I lay my requests before you and wait expectantly.
— Psalm 5:3 (NIV)

God knows our needs and what challenges we face as we travel the road of life. The ride may not always be smooth and easy, but He will give us strength and courage to follow Him wherever the road may take us. Remember, your view may be limited to what is really going on, but God knows what is around the bend.

Day of bike riding on Denali Park Road with Denali in the background, Denali National Park, Alaska

_____

_____

_____

_____

_____

_____

_____

_____

_____

Call to Me, and I will answer you, and show you great and mighty things, which you do not know.
— Jeremiah 33:3 (NKJV)

HE TOUCHES THE MOUNTAINS
Your Quiet Moments Experiencing God's Full Strength

He looks on the earth, and it trembles: He touches the mountains and they smoke. I will sing
to the Lord as long as I live: I will sing praises to my God while I have my being.
— Psalm 104:32–33 (NKJV)

I have seen many stunning sunsets as well as sunrises. The quiet of an evening as the sun slips below the horizon can feel almost like a peaceful sigh as the grandeur of a day ends. Just as refreshing is the first light of a day. The next time you enjoy a sunset or sunrise, let the palette of colors fill your eyes and let yourself feel the power of God in the quiet moment.

Winter sunrise on Illiama Volcano, Homer, Alaska

_____

_____

_____

_____

_____

_____

_____

_____

_____

_____

_____

_____

_____

_____

Winter moonrise at sunset at Tern Lake, Alaska at the Seward and Sterling Highway Junction

Praise him, sun and moon; praise him, all you shining stars. Praise him, you highest heavens and you waters above the skies. Let them praise the name of the Lord, for at his command they were created.
— Psalm 148:3–5 (NIV)

_____
_____
_____
_____
_____
_____
_____
_____
_____
_____
_____
_____
_____
_____

SILHOUETTES OF LOVE
See the Life of God's Creation Thriving All around You No Matter the Conditions Taking Place

🌿🌿🌿

The wilderness and the wasteland shall be glad for them, And the desert shall rejoice and blossom as the rose.
— Isaiah 35:1 (NKJV)

I'm certain I came to love the desert by seeing it through my dad's eyes. Some may see an unhospitable environment, but he saw the color and beauty thriving despite the harsh conditions. In trying to find a spot for a specific photo I wanted to take in Usery Mountain Park in Arizona, I almost missed the amazing view of the sun hitting the mountains behind me. While waiting for something else to happen, I almost missed another amazing photo opportunity. Are you taking time to look around at what God is trying to show you?

Staghorn Cholla blossom in the Desert Museum, Tucson, Arizona

_____

_____

_____

_____

_____

_____

_____

_____

Mountain views in Usery Mountain Regional Park, Mesa, Arizona

🍃🍃🍃

Now may the Lord direct your hearts into the love of God and into the patience of Christ.
—2 Thessalonians 3:5 (NKJV)

GOD AND THE SPEED OF LIGHT
Let God Brighten Your Darkness—and Take Time to See It

🍃🍃🍃

The Lord is my light and my salvation; Whom shall I fear? The Lord is the strength of my life; Of whom shall I be afraid?
— Psalm 27:1 (NKJV)

God's light will show you what is going on in your heart. When He brightens up the darkness, it is worth the time and effort to look at what He is showing you. Open your eyes to what He wants you to see.

Deer in woods near Gregory's Ridge Trail, Great Smoky Mountains National Park, Tennessee

_____
_____
_____
_____
_____
_____
_____
_____
_____
_____
_____

🍃🍃🍃

The day is Yours, the night also is Yours; You have prepared the light and the sun.
—Psalm 74:16 (NKJV)

HESS'S FARM
The Path of Your Life Is Constantly Touching Others.
Is God Leading You Every Moment and Step of the Way?

Yet who knows whether you have come to the kingdom for such a time as this?
—Esther 4:14 (NKJV)

My father often took me to a farm near Chillicothe, Illinois, for outdoor adventures. It was one of the more memorable places where my dad taught me about God's nature. Exploring the terrain of the valley and hills was very special to me. Those times spent with my dad ended up being a big part of what pointed me in the direction I have taken in life. What are the special times and places in your early days that factored into where you are now?

Shadow and light patterns on winter's snow, Dad's house, Lacon, Illinois

_____

_____

_____

_____

_____

_____

_____

_____

_____

_____

Blue wildflowers, Lacon, Illinois

For I know the thoughts that I think toward you, says, the Lord, thoughts of peace and not of evil,
to give you a future and a hope. Then you will call upon Me and go and pray to Me, and I will listen
to you. And you will seek Me and find Me, when you search for Me with all your heart.
—Jeremiah 29:11–13 (NKJV)

_____

_____

_____

_____

_____

_____

_____

_____

_____

_____

_____

_____

REFLECTION POND
Focus on God to Always See Amazing Things

I would have lost heart, unless I had believed that I would see the goodness of the Lord in the land of the living.
—Psalm 27:13 (NKJV)

My first two visits to Alaska were when I was just learning the ins and outs of photography. Not all pictures turned out well, but many did as I started getting the hang of using some of my new found knowledge. One of my favorites is an image of a moose I saw in Denali National Park. It wasn't totally in focus, but the picture still came out a winner. It couldn't have been clearer to me. Just like an image slightly out of focus, you don't have to clearly understand all that is going on around you to know you are seeing an amazing God in control of the world He created.

Sunrise on Denali at Reflection Pond, Denali National Park, Alaska

And he shall be like the light of the morning when the sun rises, A morning without clouds,
Like the tender grass springing out of the earth, by clear shining after rain.
—2 Samuel 23:4 (NKJV)

Eagle in flight during November Eagle Festival, Chilkat Bald Eagle Preserve, Haines, Alaska

And every creature which is in heaven and on the earth and under the earth and such as are in the sea, and all that are in them,
I heard saying: Blessing and honor and glory and power be to Him who sits on the throne, and to the Lamb, forever and ever!
— Revelation 5:13 (NKJV)

STAND IN A DIFFERENT PLACE
Allow God to Lead You for the Variety and Color He Wants You to Experience in Life

How precious also are Your thoughts to me, O God! How great is the vast sum of them! If I would count them, they are more than the sand. I awake, and I am still with you.
— Psalm 139:17–18 (ESV)

On a trip to Denali National Park, I managed to get a great shot of a fox on the colorful fall tundra. I got away from the rest of the group to see if the angle might be better. The angle wouldn't have been but, unexpectedly, the fox moved to a position right in front of me and my camera. Don't be afraid to go in a different direction than the crowd. God may surprise you with a blessing you weren't expecting.

Caribou on the fall tundra, Denali National Park, Alaska

Ground Squirrel, Denali National Park, Alaska

Honor and majesty are before Him; Strength and beauty *are* in His sanctuary.
— Psalm 96:6 (NKJV)

CAREFUL GUIDANCE
Live Life under God's Strength and Guidance Rather Than Trying to Find Your Own Way

The Lord God is my strength; He will make my feet like deer's feet, and he will make me walk on my high hills.
— Habakkuk 3:19 (NKJV)

I had to face my fear of heights during a hike in Denali National Park. I was sure I would fall down the mountainside, but the hiking guide demonstrated how sure my footing actually was. She helped me push through my fears. Although I was still nervous, I was able to enjoy the unique experience of this hike and take in the incredible beauty surrounding me. Just as I needed assistance to get down the mountain, I have learned it is better to have God's strength and guidance rather than trying to find my own way.

Greenbrier Road, Great Smoky Mountain National Park, Tennessee

_____

_____

_____

_____

_____

_____

_____

_____

_____

He who dwells in the secret place of the Most High Shall abide under the shadow of the Almighty.
I will say of the Lord, "He is my refuge and my fortress; My God, in Him I will trust."
— Psalm 91:1–2 (NKJV)

A DAY AT MENDENHALL

Spend Time Alone With God and Submerge Yourself in the Beauty of His Creation

One thing I have desired of the Lord, That will I seek: That I may dwell In the house of the Lord
All the days of my life, To behold the beauty of the Lord, and to inquire in His temple.
— Psalm 27:4 (NKJV)

We all get caught up in our day-to-day activities. We are busy with our routines, work, and families. But we need to spend quiet time alone with God each day. Not every day allows an excursion into nature, but there are many ways to spend time with God and have your daily dose of *Green Medicine*. Finding the balance isn't always easy, but don't forgo your walk in the neighborhood, or a few minutes on the deck outside. God may need to tell you something.

Mendenhall Glacier with kayakers in foreground, Juneau, Alaska

_____

_____

_____

_____

_____

_____

_____

_____

Fox on the snow at Haines Summit off the Haines Highway, Haines, Alaska

And when they were alone, He explained all things to His disciples.
— Mark 4:34 (NKJV)

_____

_____

_____

_____

_____

_____

_____

_____

_____

_____

_____

_____

_____

_____

SUNSETS WITH JORAZ
Find Moments of Peaceful Solitude in God's *Green Medicine* Every Day

Be still, and know that I am God; I will be exalted among the nations, I will be exalted in the earth.
— Psalm 46:10 (NKJV)

Home life during my teenage years was pretty rough. These were the early days of my learning about *Green Medicine* before the concept was even introduced to me. Friends of my father owned an Arabian horse named Joraz. I was fortunate to have the opportunity to help train him for several weeks while they went on vacation. The solitude of my evening rides on the country dirt roads were invaluable for the difficult times I was going through. Where do you go for your moments of peace in trying times?

Sunset over ocean and islands, Sitka, Alaska

_____

_____

_____

_____

_____

_____

_____

_____

_____

_____

Sunrise on Mt. Augustine Volcano, Homer, Alaska

The Lord will command His loving kindness in the daytime, and in the night
His song shall be with me—a prayer to the God of my life.
— Psalm 42:8 (NKJV)

THE CLEAR VIEW
Remove Interfering Distractions of Life for a Clear View of What God is Showing You

I will meditate on your precepts and contemplate your ways.
— Psalm 119:15 (NKJV)

The distractions of life can make it hard to see God. It is up to you to keep your focus on Him.
When you do, the clouds of interference will part so you can see that He is all around you.

Glacier valleys and rugged peaks of Denali and the Alaska range on flightseeing tour, Denali National Park, Alaska

_____

_____

_____

_____

_____

_____

_____

_____

_____

_____

_____

_____

_____

_____

Early summer sunset in the Upper Lynn Canal, Haines, Alaska

Your mercy, O Lord, is in the heavens; Your faithfulness reaches to the clouds. Your righteousness is like
the great mountains; Your judgments are a great deep; O Lord, You preserve man and beast.
— Psalm 36:5–6 (NKJV)

_____

_____

_____

_____

_____

_____

_____

_____

_____

_____

_____

_____

_____

_____

_____

CLOSE TO GOD

Where Is Your Special Place in Nature When You Feel Extra Close to God

O Lord, how manifold are Your works; In wisdom You have made them all. The earth is full of Your possessions.
— Psalm 104:24 (NKJV)

There's a joke I've heard that says it doesn't cost anything to call God when you are in Alaska because local calls are free. Seeing something with the magnitude of Denali or the Grand Canyon, I feel the power of how amazing God is to create something so incredibly stunning. Yet it can be found in the simpler things closer to home as well. It's beyond my imagination what it must be like to actually stand before God. What places have you felt that magnificence of God?

Denali on flightseeing tour, Denali National Park, Alaska

Who established the mountains by His strength, being clothed with power.
— Psalm 65:6 (NKJV)

MAKING GOOD OUT OF BAD

God Will Cause All Things to Work for the Good To Those That Love Him
(Romans 8:28 - NKJV)

Joseph said to them, "Do not be afraid, for am I in the place of God? But as for you, you meant evil against me; but God meant it for good, in order to bring it about as it is this day, to save many people alive."
— Genesis 50:19–20 (NKJV)

It is sometimes hard with our limited view of things to understand why things happen as they do. A flat tire, an illness, a global pandemic as well as many other situations can leave us wondering what good could come out of them. God does not cause the bad things in the world, but He can turn them into something good. As Romans 8:28 states, "God will cause all things to work for the good of *those who love Him*" (NIV; emphasis added). Joseph's brother sold him into slavery knowing he likely would not live long. However, God used that situation for His intended results. He will do the same for you.

Solar Eclipse from Brushy Mountain Trail, Great Smoky Mountains National Park, Tennessee

Piha Beach, New Zealand

🍃🍃🍃

But let him ask in faith, with no doubting, for he who doubts is like a wave of the sea driven and tossed by the wind.
— James 1:6 (NKJV)

WHAT LASTS FOREVER
God Hears And Answers Prayers When You Surrender Yourself To Him

The grass withers, the flower fades, but the word of our God stands forever.
— Isaiah 40:8 (NKJV)

I received a rather quick answer to prayer when I put a relationship completely in God's hands. I asked for it to end or for this man I loved to marry me. As it turns out, this man did ask me to marry him just five days later and, of course, I said yes. I admit, I was astonished, but knew right away it was an answer to my prayers. It doesn't always happen that way though. I have also prayed for years about being able to move to another state. There seemed to be no answer and recently, all the doors shut for this move to be possible. It doesn't mean it will never happen, but it isn't going to any time soon, if ever. Sometimes silence is your answer. No matter how fast or how long, when you surrender it all to God, he will answer your prayers and it will be what's best for you.

Redwoods in Armstrong Redwoods State Natural Reserve, California

_____

_____

_____

_____

_____

_____

For God gives wisdom and knowledge and joy to a man who is good in His sight….
— Ecclesiastes 2:26 (NKJV)

3:00 A.M. CALM
Refresh Your Soul with a Drink of God's *Green Medicine*

Be anxious for nothing, but in everything by prayer and supplication with thanksgiving let your requests be made known to God. And the peace of God, which surpasses all understanding will guard your hearts and your minds in Christ Jesus.
— Philippians 4:6–7 (NKJV)

These days, it seems so many people are very busy and are constantly on the go. I, too, am guilty of a lengthy to-do list each day. I push myself to the limits to accomplish as much as possible. But I have come to realize that God didn't intend this for us. He wants us to rest and recharge. There is no better way to do this than spending time in His creation. Whether it is a long hike or a moment to watch a sunset, let God refresh your soul with some *Green Medicine*.

Sunset on Kachemak Bay, Bishop Beach, Homer, Alaska

_____
_____
_____
_____
_____
_____
_____
_____
_____
_____
_____

Fall colors and remote cabin reflected on North Summit Lake, Seward Highway, Alaska

It is in vain that you rise up early and go late to rest, eating the bread of anxious toil; for he gives to his beloved sleep.
— Psalm 127:2 (ESV)

FORKS IN THE ROAD

God Wants What's Best for You.
Let His Direction Guide You on the Road of Life

Trust in the Lord with all your heart. And lean not on your own understanding: In
all your ways acknowledge Him, And He shall direct your paths.
— Proverbs 3:5–6 (NKJV)

I can look back and see where choices I made resulted in me sparing myself various problems. I can also look back and see that some choices weren't the best for me. I sometimes wonder what would have happened if I had chosen a different route when confronted with the fork in the road. Looking back, I have no doubt there has been divine intervention several times in my life. I am grateful for this. God is trustworthy for guiding your choices in life and He holds your future.

Slopes of mountains to the ocean on the backside of the Road to Hana, Maui, Hawaii

_____
_____
_____
_____
_____
_____
_____
_____
_____
_____

Fall colors along Seward Highway near Hope, Alaska.

He found him in a desert land, and in the wasteland, a howling wilderness; He encircled him,
He instructed him, He kept him as the apple of His eye…so the Lord alone led him.
— Deuteronomy 32:10 & 12 (NKJV)

_____
_____
_____
_____
_____
_____
_____
_____
_____
_____
_____
_____
_____
_____
_____

THUNDERSTORMS
Finding Peace in Your Heart When Storms Rage Around You

The rain came down, the streams rose, and the winds blew and beat against that
house; yet it did not fall, because it had its foundation on the rock.
— Matthew 7:25 (NIV)

I love thunderstorms. They don't happen too often in Alaska, so when I am in the lower 48 and get to
experience one, I marvel at the power of nature. I used to watch them with my father in the safety of our
home or garage. We enjoyed the security of our vantage point while the storm outside raged. Just as I felt
safe with my father, I have peace inside during tumultuous times because I know God is with me.

Raindrops on fall colored leaves, Glacier National Park, Montana

_____

_____

_____

_____

_____

_____

_____

There will be a tabernacle for shade in the daytime from the heat, for a place of refuge, and for shelter from storm and rain.
— Isaiah 4:6 (NKJV)

EAGLE FESTIVAL
Run On the Strength of God in Life, Not Your Own Power

🍃🍃🍃

But those who hope in the Lord will renew their strength. They will soar on wings like
eagles; they will run, and not grow weary, they will walk and not be faint.
— Isaiah 40:31 (NIV)

Haines, Alaska is known for several unique attributes. One that stands out is the gathering of the eagles on the Chilkat River each fall. A late run of salmon creates a concentrated food source and thousands of eagles show up for the bountiful feast. My job there came with a lot of stress, but just like the wind beneath the wings of an eagle, God gave me strength to carry the load.

Eagle in flight over Chilkat River in Chilkat Bald Eagle Preserve, Haines, Alaska

_____

_____

_____

_____

_____

_____

_____

_____

_____

_____

_____

_____

Bald Eagle on snowy banks of Chilkat River in November, Haines, Alaska

Praise the Lord, my soul, and forget not all his benefits…who satisfied your desires
with good things so that your youth is renewed like the eagle's.
— Psalm 103:2 and 5 (NIV)

ILLINOIS RIVER WITH DAD
Make Sure God Is the Influence on the Flow of the River of Your Life

You visit the earth and water it, You greatly enrich it; The river of God is full of water; You provide their grain, For so You have prepared it. You water its ridges abundantly, You settle its furrows; You make it soft with showers, You bless its growth.
— Psalm 65:9–10 (NKJV)

There is no question that my father embedded in me a deep appreciation for nature. As a small child, he spent time with me in God's creation passing along his knowledge of the great outdoors. We often went for walks along the Illinois River where he told me about the ecology as well as the economy of the river. The course of my own river of life was greatly influenced by him with the source springing from God. Who has influenced the flow of your river in life?

Fall colors on the Chilkat River, Haines, Alaska

_____

_____

_____

_____

_____

_____

_____

_____

All the rivers run into the sea, yet the sea is not full; To the place from which the rivers come, there they return again.
— Ecclesiastes 1:7 (NKJV)

WHAT ABOUT ME?
THE CHOICE IS MINE
Ground Yourself and Your Children in a Foundation of God for the Best Choices in Life

Your word is a lamp to my feet and a light to my path.
— Psalm 119:105 (NKJV)

You can't help what hand you were dealt in life, but the choice is yours as to how you will play it. There are things in my life that were out of my control and which I wish had not happened to me. Such things can set a person's course in life. For one person, it can be his or her demise. For another, it becomes a source of motivation. It's up to you to decide and allow God to lead you on the best path possible. He will if you let Him.

Fall colors on the Alcan Highway near Toad River, British Columbia, Canada

_____

_____

_____

_____

_____

_____

_____

_____

_____

_____

Rainbow over ocean as tour boat heads out from Maalaea Harbor, Maui, Hawaii

Fear not, for I am with you: Be not dismayed, for I am your God. I will strengthen you,
Yes, I will help you, I will uphold you with My righteous right hand.
— Isaiah 41:10 (NKJV)

THINGS WE SAY
The Power of Words Can Change the Landscape of Others around You

But I tell you that for every careless word that people speak, they will give an account of it on the day of judgement.
— Matthew 12:36 (NASB)

My father said something very damaging to one of my brothers. In a matter of seconds, words were uttered that inflicted a wound that has lasted years. Despite the circumstances of why the incident occurred, there was no justification to the heart that has carried it from then on. Words can have lasting, detrimental effects on those around you or can raise them to new heights. Are you bulldozing your landscape or preserving the best view for others?

Prickly Pear Cactus bloom at the Desert Museum, Tucson, Arizona

Let the words of my mouth and the meditation of my heart be acceptable in your sight, O Lord, my rock and my Redeemer.
— Psalm 19:14 (NKJV)

_____
_____
_____
_____
_____
_____
_____
_____
_____

Bee on Wild Geranium along the Russian River, Cooper Landing, Alaska

Gracious words are like a honeycomb, sweetness to the soul and health to the body.
— Proverbs 16:24 (ESV)

_____
_____
_____
_____
_____
_____
_____
_____
_____
_____
_____
_____
_____
_____
_____
_____
_____

MAY THE LORD BLESS YOU AND KEEP YOU
Pray for God to Bless and Keep Your Family and Friends

The Lord bless you and keep you; The Lord make His face shine upon you, And be gracious
to you; The Lord lift up His countenance upon you, and give you peace.
—Numbers 6: 24–26 (ESV)

This verse was recited to me by my father as a nightly ritual when tucking me into bed as a little girl. It often
appeared in letters and communication I had with him as an adult. It's a good verse and prayer to hang on to
no matter how old you are. Pray diligently for the Lord to bless and keep your loved ones and friends.

Bull moose lying down on fall-colored ridge at Reflection Pond, Denali National Park, Alaska

Seagulls on beach, Sarasota, Florida

When you lie down, you will not be afraid; Yes, you will lie down and your sleep will be sweet.
— Proverbs 3:24 (NKJV)

LOVE OF FLOWERS

Stop and Notice the Flowers, Taking Time to Enjoy the World God Created

Many, O Lord my God, are Your wonderful works which You have done; And Your thoughts toward us cannot be recounted to You in order; If I would declare and speak of them, they are more than can be numbered.
— Psalm 40:5 (NKJV)

My father loved flowers. He appreciated their beauty. I often shared my flower photographs with him, so it was difficult after he passed with so many images on hand reminding me of him. But the sadness of missing him eased as I let flowers become a happy remembrance of my dad. Flowers to me now are a reminder of *Green Medicine* scattered everywhere.

Fireweed blossoms on Bishop Beach, Homer, Alaska

Squirrel Corn blossom on Porter's Creek Trail, Greenbrier, Smoky Mountains National Park, Tennessee

You will keep him in perfect peace, whose mind is stayed on You because he trusts in You.
— Isaiah 26:3 (NKJV)

FRESH BEGINNINGS
God Will Refresh Your Heart and Soul Like New With the Resources of His Creation

In the beginning, Lord, you laid the foundations of the earth and the heavens are the work of your hands.
— Hebrews 1:10 (NKJV)

My honeymoon was spent in Hawaii, where my husband and I took unforgettable drive on the Road to Hana. Stopping many times along the way to learn the history and take in the sights, it was one of the more remarkable days in my life. There were many waterfalls to view along the drive. I found them quite revitalizing on such a hot day. Just as God sustains the earth with the waters that flow, Maui was a good watering of the souls at the start of a wonderful marriage.

Rainbow on backside of Road to Hana, Maui, Hawaii

_____

_____

_____

_____

_____

_____

_____

_____

_____

_____

He gives rain on the earth, and sends waters on the fields.
— Job 5:10 (NKJV)

A THOUSAND SPRINGS

Let the Maintenance of Your Life Be Handled by the Precision Only God Can Provide

I know that everything God does, It shall be forever; nothing can be added to it and nothing can be taken from it.
— Ecclesiastes 3:14 (NKJV)

We are all delicate human beings in need of the special maintenance only provided by God. Our hearts and souls must be in good working order for us to be useful instruments for Him. Just like the clockmaker handles the inner workings of a clock, how God nurtures the intricacy of our lives may very well be maintained through His *Green Medicine.*

Lower part of Laurel Falls, Great Smoky Mountains National Park, Tennessee

Ramsey Cascades in mist, Greenbrier, Smoky Mountains National Park, Tennessee

For we are his workmanship, created in Christ Jesus for good works, which
God prepared beforehand that we should walk in them.
— Ephesians 2:10 (NKJV)

RAINBOWS
Like the Rainbow Reminds Us, Have No Doubt God Keeps His Promises

I have set my rainbow in the clouds, and it will be the sign of the covenant between me and the earth.
— Genesis 9:13 (NIV)

Rainbows are signs to all that God keeps His promises. This should bring you peace, wash over you like a spring rain, and brighten your day. Remember the times you've seen rainbows and reflect on how they made you feel. Is it different when you think of God's promise?

Rainbow over Kachemak Bay from East End Road, Homer, Alaska

_____
_____
_____
_____
_____
_____
_____
_____
_____
_____
_____

Rainbow over small cruise ship in Lynn Canal, Alaska

Like the appearance of a rainbow in a cloud on a rainy day, so was the appearance of the brightness all around it. This was the appearance of the likeness of the glory of the Lord.
— Ezekiel 1:28 (NKJV)

MUSIC AND JOY
Each Day Is a Gift from God. Take Pleasure in Living the Life He's Given You and Be Thankful.

The Lord is my strength and my shield; my heart trusts in him, and He helps
me. My heart leaps for joy, and with my song I praise Him.
— Psalm 28:7 (NIV)

Music is a mental photograph of emotions for a time and place. There is a CD that I listened to when I was driving the Alcan Highway. Every time I hear one of those songs, it takes me back to the sights I saw on the drive and the free feeling I had driving through the spectacular, remote scenery. My father loved music and, surprisingly, a variety of genres. We often shared music with each other and discussed the artists we enjoyed. We frequently listened to our favorites on drives or looking out the window as we talked. What music has captured some of your favorite *Green Medicine* experiences?

Butterfly on Fairy Duster in Desert Botanical Gardens, Phoenix, Arizona

_____

_____

_____

_____

_____

_____

_____

_____

_____

_____

Fall colors and Glacier National Park Mountains from St. Mary's, Montana

Behold, God is my salvation, I will trust and not be afraid; For the Lord Jehovah
is my strength and my song; He also has become my salvation.
— Isaiah 12:2 (AKJV)

_____
_____
_____
_____
_____
_____
_____
_____
_____
_____
_____
_____
_____
_____
_____
_____

THE SUN KNOWS ITS SETTING
Favorite Sunsets and Who You Share Them With

Let the name of the Lord be praised, both now and forevermore. From the rising of the sun to the place where it sets, the name of the Lord is to be praised. The Lord is exalted over all the nations, His glory above the heavens.
— Psalm 113:2–4 (NIV)

On a cold winter evening while visiting my father, the colors of the sky caught our attention on our way to dinner. We stopped to catch a few minutes of the sunset. I recall the temperature being in the teens with the wind blowing. It was cold. But in those moments of viewing that sunset, two photos were taken and the memory has never faded. Write about some of your favorite sunset memories and who you shared them with.

Sunset over Cook Inlet and Mount Douglas, Homer, Alaska

_____

_____

_____

_____

_____

_____

_____

_____

_____

_____

_____

Sunset over the Chilkat Valley, Haines, Alaska

The Mighty One, God the Lord, Has spoken and called the earth from the rising of the sun
to its going down. Out of Zion, the perfection of beauty, God will shine forth.
— Psalm 50:1–2 (NKJV)

_____
_____
_____
_____
_____
_____
_____
_____
_____
_____
_____
_____
_____
_____
_____
_____
_____

SIGNIFICANT IN VASTNESS

Like All Details in Nature, God Took Time to Create You.
You Are a Significant Part of His Handiwork

When I consider Your heavens, the work of Your fingers, The moon and the stars, which You have ordained, What is man that you are mindful of him, and the son of man that You visit him? For You have made him a little lower than the angels, And you have crowned him with glory and honor.
—Psalm 8:3–5 (NKJV)

To me, there is nothing like looking at the night sky to make me feel small while feeling the greatness of God. The world is huge but the universe is unfathomable in size. I'm just a speck within it. But I still matter to God. So do you. We are valuable to Him and his purpose. Thank God for the incredible beauty and truth nature and the heavens reveal about Him and know He cares for you.

Berner's Bay near Haines, Lynn Canal, Alaska

_____
_____
_____
_____
_____
_____
_____

Caribou alone on fall-colored tundra, Denali National Park, Alaska

He counts the number of the stars; He calls them all by name. Great is our
Lord, and mighty in power; His understanding is infinite.
—Psalm 147:4–5 (NKJV)

THE CHOICES YOU MAKE
Your Choices Impact You and All around You. Make Sure God Is Guiding Those Decisions.

❦❦❦

You will show me the path of life; In Your presence is fullness of joy; At Your right hand are pleasures forevermore.
—Psalm 16:11 (NKJV)

Going through a box of old family photos at my grandmother's one day, I came across an intriguing image of a relative I had never known. My grandmother filled me in on his sad story. However, the image I held in my hand captured a happier moment in his life. I don't know all the details, but the woman in the photograph who caused his expression of contentment was not the one he ended up marrying. I may never know what might have been if I had made different choices as I've traveled through life. However, I am certain that as a Christian, God will intervene on the direction your life takes. I know He has for me. Are you factoring in God for your decisions? Be thankful for His guiding hand.

Alaska Highway heading towards Haines Junction, Yukon Territory, Canada

Kayakers near Aialik Glacier, Kenai Fjords National Park, Alaska

❦ ❦ ❦

And whatever you do in word or deed, do all in the name of the Lord Jesus, giving thanks to God the Father through Him.
—Colossians 3:17 (NKJV)

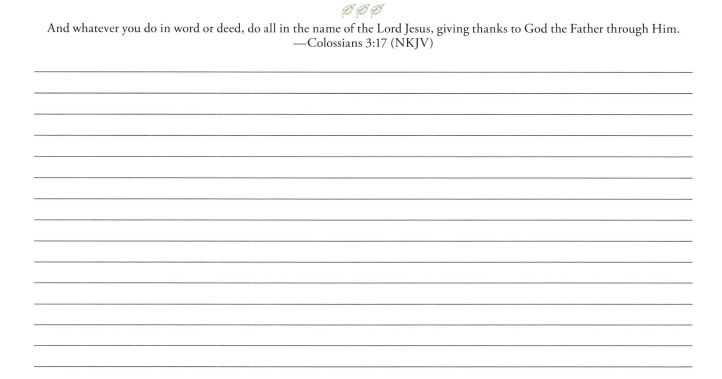

CARRYING GOD'S WATER

Do You Fit into the Plans God Wants to Accomplish? Be like the Rain He Sends to Nourish the Earth.

So shall My word be that goes forth from My mouth; It shall not return to Me void, but it shall accomplish what I please, and it shall prosper *in the thing* for which I sent it. For you shall go out with joy and be led out with peace; The mountains and the hills shall break forth into singing before you, and all the trees of the field shall clap their hands.
—Isaiah 55:11–12 (NKJV)

Rain provides sustenance that allows life on our planet to thrive. Without rain, life withers and dies. We can never know the plans God has for this world. His perspective is from a much different vantage point than ours. It is better to fit into His plans than try to mold Him into ours. Like rain nourishing the earth, let Him use you to touch the lives of others.

Dew drop on Dryopteric Wood Fern on Little River Trail, Elkmont area of Great Smoky Mountains National Park, Tennessee

_____
_____
_____
_____
_____
_____
_____
_____

But whoever drinks of the water that I shall give him will never thirst. But the water that I shall give him will become in him a fountain of water springing up into everlasting life.
—John 4:14 (NKJV)

BEING THANKFUL
There Are Blessings from God Every Day.
Be Thankful To Him for All He Provides to You.

When you have eaten and are full, then you shall bless the Lord your God for the good land which He has given you.
—Deuteronomy 8:10 (NKJV)

Every meal should be an occasion for thanksgiving. We should have gratitude toward God at the beginning of the meal for the food we have to eat as well at the end for being full and satisfied. Not everyone is so blessed. Don't forget to be grateful to God for his goodness and all He provides to you each day.

Sunrise over Chilkat Mountains, Haines, Alaska

_____
_____
_____
_____
_____
_____
_____
_____
_____
_____

Therefore, whether you eat or drink or whatever you do, do all to the glory of God.
—1 Corinthians 10:31 (NKJV)

STRENGTH

God Will Give You Strength to Accomplish All He Wants You to Do. Draw On the Reservoir of His Power.

I can do all things through Christ who strengthens me.
—Philippians 4:13 (NKJV)

There are times I am not sure how I will deal with situations in life. They can wear me down. My enthusiasm fades at times. We all need rest to recharge. It may not always be easy, but trust God's timing. Take heart in knowing He is never too busy to listen. Draw on the reservoir of His power. He will give you what you need to accomplish what needs to be done.

Eagle in Flight in Chilkat Bald Eagle Preserve, Haines, Alaska

_____
_____
_____
_____
_____
_____
_____
_____
_____
_____
_____

Snow machining at Haines Summit, Yukon Territory, Canada

I lift up my eyes to the hills—where does my help come from? My help comes from the Lord, the Maker of heaven and earth.
—Psalm 121:1–2 (NIV)

_____
_____
_____
_____
_____
_____
_____
_____
_____
_____
_____
_____
_____
_____
_____
_____
_____
_____

COMPASSION
Until Your Heart Stops Beating, God's Not Done with You.
Let God Use You and Others to the Very End

You gave me life and showed me kindness, and in your providence watched over my spirit.
—Job 10:12 (NIV)

The passing of my mother-in-law was a difficult period for me, but especially for my husband. There was nothing the doctors could do for her, so it was a matter of letting nature take its course. She was able to die in her own home, but the process was agonizingly slow. Many of us, myself included, questioned why God didn't just take her quickly and end the suffering. Through this, I learned that God's timing is impeccable. As I watched family come and go, new relationships develop and others mend, I realized He was using this woman to the very last second. By the end, I had a new grasp on the meaning of compassion. Who was I to decide how God should work out what He needed to in the hearts of so many? Until your heart stops beating, God's not done with you yet.

Saguaros silhouetted at sunset in Usery Mountain Park, Mesa, Arizona

_____

_____

_____

_____

_____

_____

_____

_____

_____

Foam Flower blossoms along Little River Trail, Elkmont, Great Smoky Mountains National Park, Tennessee

Therefore, as the elect of God, holy and beloved, put on tender mercies, kindness, humility, meekness, longsuffering, bearing with one another, and forgiving one another, if anyone has a complaint against another; even as Christ forgave you, so you also must do. But above all these things put on love, which is the bond of perfection.
—Colossians 3:12–14 (NKJV)

GOD'S PURPOSE

Stay Faithful and Calm Regardless of the Turmoil Around You

And we know that all things work together for good to those who love God,
to those who are the called according to *His* purpose.
—Romans 8:28 (NKJV)

In the last days of my mother-in-law's life, things became very stressful for my husband. We didn't know how long she might hang on and at times, it seemed it could be months. Figuring out what to do with her finances, long-term care, her home, and belongings were all factoring into the strain of the situation. We were trying to make it all work according to how *we* thought it should be. One night, we found peace when we just resigned the situation to God. When it was the right time, He would take her. How we would manage the details would be taken day by day. We just turned it over to Him. God used my mother-in-law to teach me and my husband a lesson in trust and patience.

Sunset over Cook Inlet, Anchorage, Alaska

Kachemak Bay and Homer Bluffs seen from the Homer Spit, Homer, Alaska

Cause me to hear Your lovingkindness in the morning, For in You do I trust; Cause me
to know the way in which I should walk, For I lift up my soul to You.

LIGHT TO SEE THE DARKNESS

Let the Light of God Show You the Pitfalls to Avoid in Life

For You will light my lamp: The Lord my God will enlighten my darkness.
—Psalm 18:28 (NKJV)

Light reveals shadowy dark areas. Your vehicle's headlights not only help you see where you are going, they allow you to see the holes and damaged areas to avoid with contrasting darkness. Letting God shine His light in your heart may expose the compromised places in your life. Allow God to shine full force on you so you can navigate safely in this world.

Eldred Rock Lighthouse in Lynn Canal, Haines, Alaska

Kenai Mountains and Kenai Lake with fall colors, Cooper Landing, Alaska

For God, who said, "Let light shine out of darkness," made his light shine in our hearts to
give us the light of the knowledge of God's glory displayed in the face of Christ.
—2 Corinthians 4:6 (NIV)

A PERFECT DAY
Let Your Attitude Be Shaped By God for More Perfect Days Ahead

But the path of the just is like the shining sun, That shines ever brighter unto the perfect day.
—Proverbs 4:18 (NKJV)

I have had several days I consider perfect. Don't get me wrong. Not every moment of every day is flowers and mountains and beautiful scenes of nature. Not every day is easy for me. When it seems like things are going wrong, I know I need to refocus. When that focus gets back on track with God, I get through and find peace because I have faith that He is truly in control despite any challenges. It's a choice to trust God. And that kind of thinking means a perfect day could be just a thought away. What are the days you remember and may have deemed perfect?

Mt. Augustine Volcano silhouetted against sunset on Cook Inlet, Homer, Alaska

_____
_____
_____
_____
_____
_____
_____
_____
_____
_____
_____
_____
_____

Eagles in early morning mist over Chilkat River, Haines, Alaska

I will meditate on the glorious splendor of Your Majesty and on Your wondrous works.
—Psalm 145:5 (NKJV)

STRETCH OUT THE HEAVENS
Look To the Skies and Know That God is the Amazing Creator of Everything in the Universe

Bless the Lord, O my soul! O Lord my God, You are very great; You are clothed with honor and majesty.
Who cover Yourself with light as with a garment, Who stretch out the heavens like a curtain.
—Psalm 104:1–2 (NKJV)

I lived in Homer, Alaska, two times. The second time, I was there through the winter. The home I rented was on a hill with a great view of the Kachemak Bay and the Homer Spit. It was also rather dark around there, which was perfect for searching the night skies for northern lights, or aurora borealis. If clear skies were in the forecast, I would set my alarm clock for every hour to see if they were out. And if they were, I had things set up with my camera so all I had to do was step outside my door and take the pictures. There were times it was simply breathtaking. I would watch them dance across the night sky and think about how big the universe is and how amazing God is to have created it.

Northern Lights over Homer, Alaska

Sunset on the Smoky Mountains, Clingman's Dome, Great Smoky Mountains National Park, Tennessee

Let the heavens rejoice, and let the earth be glad: and let them say among the nations, "The Lord reigns."
—1 Chronicles 16:31 (NKJV)

_____
_____
_____
_____
_____
_____
_____
_____
_____
_____
_____
_____
_____
_____
_____
_____

RIVERS FLOW BETWEEN MOUNTAINS
Study God's Word and Let It Flow Through You

"Whoever believes in Me as the Scripture has said, out of his heart will flow rivers of living water."
—John 7:38 (NKJV)

Any body of water will find its way no matter the obstacle. If there is some obstruction in a stream or river, a path over or around will develop. God is the river that overcomes everything. When I study His word and concentrate on Him, His living waters flow through me. No obstacle will ever be too much to deal with. Be a tributary of God and let Him flow through you to overcome the obstacles and touch countless lives. The current of your life will stay steady if you go with His flow.

Fall colors over Russian River, Cooper Landing, Alaska

_____

_____

_____

_____

_____

_____

_____

_____

_____

_____

_____

Waterfall along Rhododendron Trail, Greenbrier, Great Smoky Mountains National Park, Tennessee

Now it shall come to pass in the latter days that the mountain of the Lord's house shall be established on the top of the mountains and shall be exalted above the hills; and all nations shall flow to it.
—Isaiah 2:2 (NKJV)

DENALI
Be Awestruck By God and All He Has Created

🍃🍃🍃

Oh, worship the Lord in the beauty of holiness! Tremble before Him, all the earth.
—Psalm 96:9 (NKJV)

I was inspired to write my Denali song upon my first visit to Denali National Park. Seeing the mountain for the first time moved me like nothing I have ever experienced. It has that effect on people. Even seeing it numerous times after and occasionally in the distance from my home in Anchorage, it still calls to me. Take time to think about what really inspires you. From the grandest of mountains to the smallest details of nature, what *Green Medicine* have you encountered that moves you like nothing else you ever faced?

Foxtail, Homer, Alaska

_____

_____

_____

_____

_____

_____

_____

_____

_____

_____

Denali and the Alaska Range, Denali National Park, Alaska

The mountains will bring peace to the people, and the little hills, by righteousness.
—Psalm 72:3 (NKJV)

THE LAST LETTER
Be an Inspiration for Having a Foundation in Christ and Share God's *Green Medicine* With Others

That they may see and know, And consider and understand together, that the hand
of the Lord has done this, and the Holy One of Israel has created it.
—Isaiah 41:20 (NKJV)

In my *Green Medicine* book, I have a hard time reading my own entry about the last letter I ever received from
my father. I long for more opportunities to see him and talk to him. I have no regrets other than wishing I had
made the journey back to visit more often or made another attempt to call before he died. You never know
when the last time will be the last. Don't let there be regret. Let those around you know they are loved.
I miss my father very much, but I am very grateful he showed me the *Green Medicine* in God's creation.

Sunrise over Chilkat Mountains, Haines, Alaska

While I live I will praise the Lord; I will sing praises to my God while I have my being.
—Psalm 146:2 (NKJV)

_____

_____

_____

_____

_____

_____

_____

Sunset on Denali, Reflection Pond, Denali National Park, Alaska

"And if I go and prepare a place for you, I will come back and take you to be with me that you also may be where I am."
—John 14:3 (NIV)

ABOUT THE AUTHOR AND HER PHOTOGRAPHY

I was born in Peoria, Illinois. My early years were spent growing up in Chillicothe, Illinois, a little community on the Illinois River. After living in various towns and cities in the state, I moved on to Gatlinburg, Tennessee, not long after I graduated from high school. For the most part, I spent the next twenty years living in the Smoky Mountains region. When I was thirty-four, I chased my dream to drive to and live in Alaska. I currently reside in Anchorage, Alaska with my husband Ed.

A lot of people have inquired about my photo skills. If you are into photography at all, you always get a little jolted when someone comments, "Your pictures are so good. You must have a good camera." I've never thought of myself as a professional photographer, but there's more to it than a good camera. As noted, though, in my *Green Medicine* book, my photography skills were self-taught in the years leading up to my first visit to Alaska.

I started my relationship with the photography world with a Maxxum 7000 camera a friend gave to me. After whetting my appetite with that model, I splurged and moved up to the Minolta Maxxum 9. I joined a camera club and a few members recommended specific photography books to learn camera settings. I wish I still had those books or at least remembered the names of them as I wouldn't mind purchasing them again. They were great tools for understanding the basics and learning the desired image settings. How I miss the days of 35 mm film. Give me some luscious colors of Fuji Velvia and I could be in heaven for hours outside on the trails.

I wanted to get the hang of understanding how the adjustments of aperture and shutter speed would affect the picture I was taking. To learn the camera and how to manipulate it for the desired outcome of an image, I would head out into the "field" of the Smoky Mountains with notepad and pen or a small tape-recording device. I would make notes of the settings for each frame I was shooting in various light and subject matter. Those were the days of film, so the results of my effort were not instantaneous as they are now with digital cameras. It was tedious, but I found it extremely enjoyable to get rolls of film back in the mail, see the images I shot, and go over my notes. I truly learned a lot of the photography fundamentals this way.

As the digital world took over the camera and film industry, I eventually gave in and got my first digital camera, a Nikon D50. I loved that little thing and still have it. It needs a little professional attention for the auto-focus, but it can still be used as is.

I am currently still in the stages of developing my relationship with my latest addition to the camera family, a Nikon D7500. There is much to learn with all these new cameras can do and how to get the menu settings configured to your liking. It takes study with the manual, but I have found it mostly just requires spending quality time with the equipment in the various elements.

My advice to any of you wanting to document your own *Green Medicine* adventures with images, even with the digital techniques of the day, is study your camera in the manner I did with my first film camera. Find things you want to photograph and take multiple shots with different apertures and shutter speeds while making notes about the settings of each frame. When you are looking at them on the big monitor of your computer with your photo software, you will make the connection with what you've done and see the effects. This will help you get to know your equipment better. Like anything else, if you practice, the skill becomes second nature. The more time you spend with your camera, the more it becomes a friend you work well with. I won't lie: it's not uncommon to take numerous pictures of the same thing and only one image comes out well, or even none. But the more prepared you are with the functionality of your gear, the better your odds for great images. When that great shot comes along and the light is changing fast or the animal is on the move, you will be able to jump into action and have better chance of getting images you want.

You can have the finest camera, the fanciest gear, and the best accessories to go with it, but the real secret to getting good photographs is to simply be there. You have to be where the wildlife is or the scenic vistas are, and know where to go for the best view of the sunset. Make time to hit the trails and go for the drives or pull out that kayak. However you like to do it, whether your interest is in photography or the experience of a place, just get out there and enjoy what God has given us in His creation.

I've been blessed to find a way to live in some places of extraordinary beauty where I could simply look out my front window or step out my door to take in the magnificent natural beauty of where I lived. My life in Anchorage, Alaska, can still allow for that, but not quite as easily as other places I've lived in this great state. The past few years have been filled with my full-time job, a home, a husband, and solidifying the dream of my books. But there's a lot of *Green Medicine* to share and there is likely more of it to come.

THE SINNER'S PRAYER

Dear Lord Jesus, I know that I am a sinner, and I ask for Your forgiveness. I believe You died for my sins and rose from the dead. I turn from my sins and invite You to come into my heart and life. I want to trust and follow You as my Lord and Savior.